Present and Speaking Everywhere:

A Collection of Found Poetry/Art

by

Jennifer Rood

Published in the United States by
Not a Pipe Publishing, Independence, Oregon.
www.NotAPipePublishing.com

Paperback Edition

ISBN-13: 978-1-956892-42-0

Cover by Jennifer Rood

This book is a collection of works of art created by the poet. Source text for the found poetry created here came from various places, including books, newspapers, a magazine, a newsletter, and a poem. Specific texts include: *The Contrarians* by Gary Sernovitz, *How to Keep Bees* by Anna Botsford Comstock, the *Grants Pass Daily Courier*, *The Wall Street Journal*, *Better Homes and Gardens*, *Oregon Masonic News*, and "In Reference to Her Children" by Anne Bradstreet. The poet attests all works are transformative because they have entirely different purposes than the original works and are therefore not violations of copyright in accordance with *Cariou v. Prince*, 714 F.3d 694 (2d Cir. 2013).

Present and Speaking Everywhere

Preface

The pieces of found poetry and art you see in these pages began emerging during the depths of the Covid-19 pandemic. Finding hidden messages of hope and positivity in the words around me gave me a way to cope with the great swaths of time that opened up when everything else shut down, and also a way to counteract the stress and fear that came with lockdown. Once I started creating these pieces, I found it hard to stop. I especially loved the linguistic challenge of linking words together combined with the artistic challenge of building images around those words. For the less visually complex pieces, I simply enjoyed the meditative process of obscuring the words that didn't belong with pen or paint (or whatever other media struck me at the time as appropriate or interesting). Either way, I got satisfaction out of producing something tangible every day or two during a time when each day blended into each nondescript next. It kept me curious as I wondered what my next discovery might be.

Perhaps, then, it is no surprise that I have arranged the poems in this collection to take the reader on a journey that begins with the simple truth that "poetry is present and speaking everywhere." Although each page, each poem, can be considered on its own, the book is also designed to be read as a unified whole. If you read the book straight through in one sitting, you can experience the subtle narrative thread that stitches through the stages of seeking and finding. There are poems about curiosity and questioning, poems about leaving yesterday behind to find what tomorrow might bring, poems about seeking peace and finding joy, and poems about choosing to engage with the world with a sense of love and caring for all of humanity, for all of nature, for "all of it." The book ends with an acknowledgment that time is short, and with a wish that you, the reader, "remain open and fill your life with joy."

We are all on our own journeys of seeking and finding. May you travel well.

—Jennifer Rood

poetry

is

t and presen-
speaking everywhere

Poetry
is
present
and
speaking
everywhere.

Is it upon mature consideration we adopt the idea, that nature is thus partial in her distributions? Is it indeed a fact, that she hath yielded to one half of the human species so unquestionable a mental superiority? I know that to both sexes elevated understandings, and the reverse, are common. But, suffer me to ask, in what the minds of females are so notoriously deficient, or unfair. May not the intellectual powers be ranged under these four heads—imagination, reason, memory and judgment. The province of imagination hath long since been surrendered up to us, and we have been crowned undoubted sovereigns of the regions of fancy. Invention is perhaps the most arduous effort of the mind; this branch of imagination hath been particularly ceded to us, and we have been time out of mind invested with that creative faculty. Observe the variety of fashions (here I bar the contemptuous smile) which distinguish and adorn the female world; how continually are they changing, insomuch that they almost render the wise man's assertion problematical, and we are ready to say *there is something new under the sun*. Now what a playfulness, what an exuberance of fancy, what strength of inventive imagination, doth this continual variation discover? Again, it hath been observed, that if the turpitude of the conduct of our sex, hath been ever so enormous, so extremely ready are we, that the very first thought presents us with an apology so plausible, as to produce our actions even in an amiable light. Another instance of our creative powers, is our talent for slander; how ingenious are we at inventive scandal? what a formidable story can we in a moment fabricate merely from the force of a prolifick imagination? how many reputations, in the fertile brain of a female, have been utterly despoiled? how industrious are we at improving a hint? suspicion how easily do we convert into conviction, and conviction embellished by the power of eloquence, stalks abroad to the surprise and confusion of unsuspecting innocence. Perhaps it will be asked if I furnish these facts as instances of excellency in our sex. Certainly not, but as proofs of a creative faculty, of a lively imagination. Assuredly great activity of mind is thereby discovered, and was this activity properly directed, what beneficial effects would follow. Is the needle and kitchen sufficient to employ the operations of a soul thus organized? I should conceive not. Nay, it is a truth that those very departments leave the intelligent principle vacant, and at liberty for speculation. Are we deficient in reason? we can only reason from what we know, and if an opportunity of acquiring knowledge hath been denied us, the inferiority of our sex cannot fairly be deduced from thence. Memory, I believe, will be allowed us in common, since every one's experience must testify, that a loquacious old woman is as frequently met with, as a communicative old man; their subjects are alike drawn from the fund of other times, and the transactions of their youth, or of maturer life, entertain, or perhaps fatigue you, in the evening of

Imagination is mind

invested
with playfulness
ready
to discover.

wake up tomorrow

just wondering,

question

question

question

question,

invigorating,

beautiful

maddening questions

Wake up tomorrow
just wondering...

question   ?

?   question

question   ?

question—

invigorating, beautiful,
maddening questions!

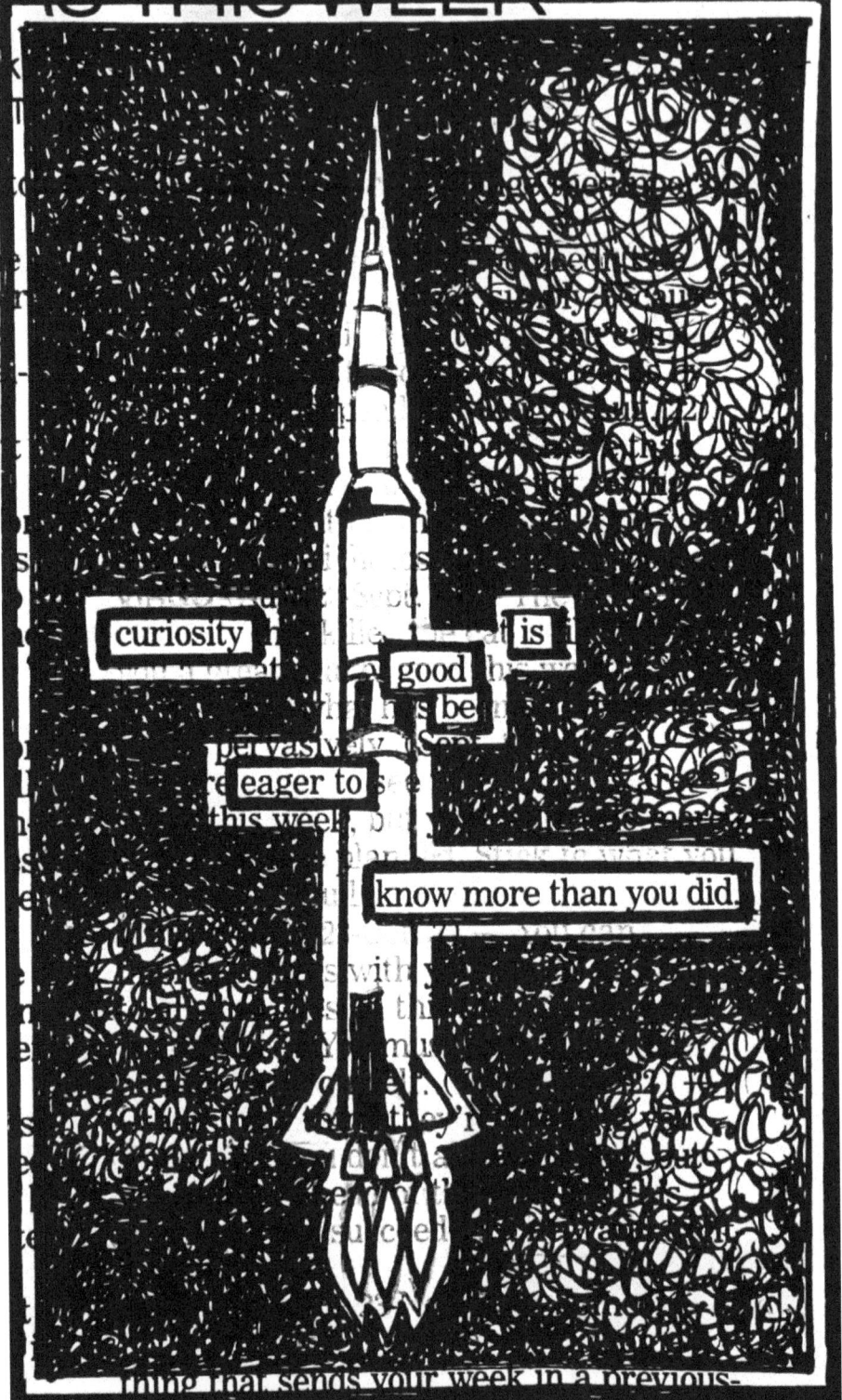

curiosity is good be eager to know more than you did.

Curiosity
is good;
be eager
to know more
than you did.

the goal isn't to be still willing to plunge in

The goal
isn't
to be still—

be willing
to plunge in!

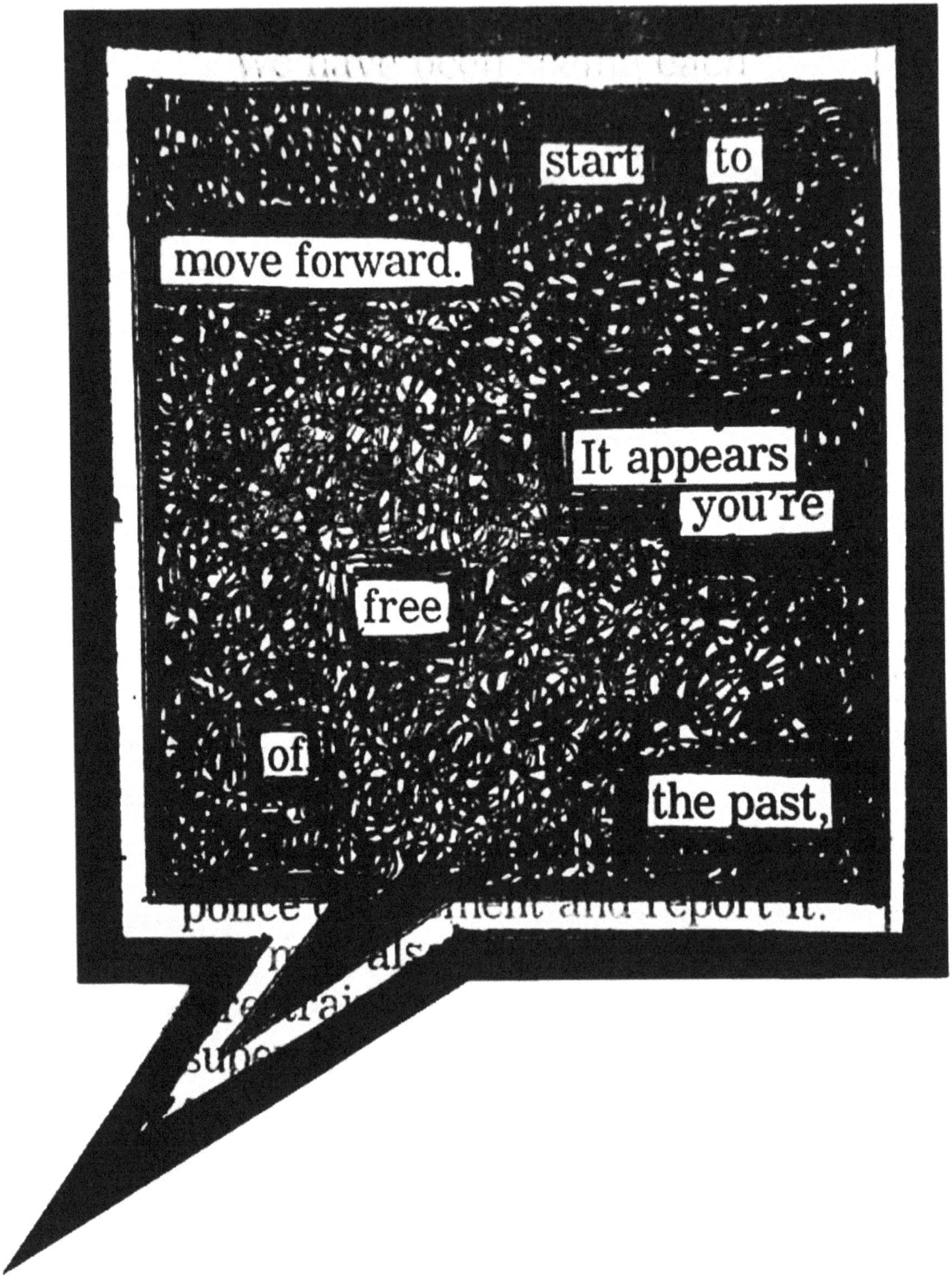
start to
move forward.
It appears
you're
free
of
the past,

Start to move forward.

It appears
you're free
of the past.

A desired past
is useless.

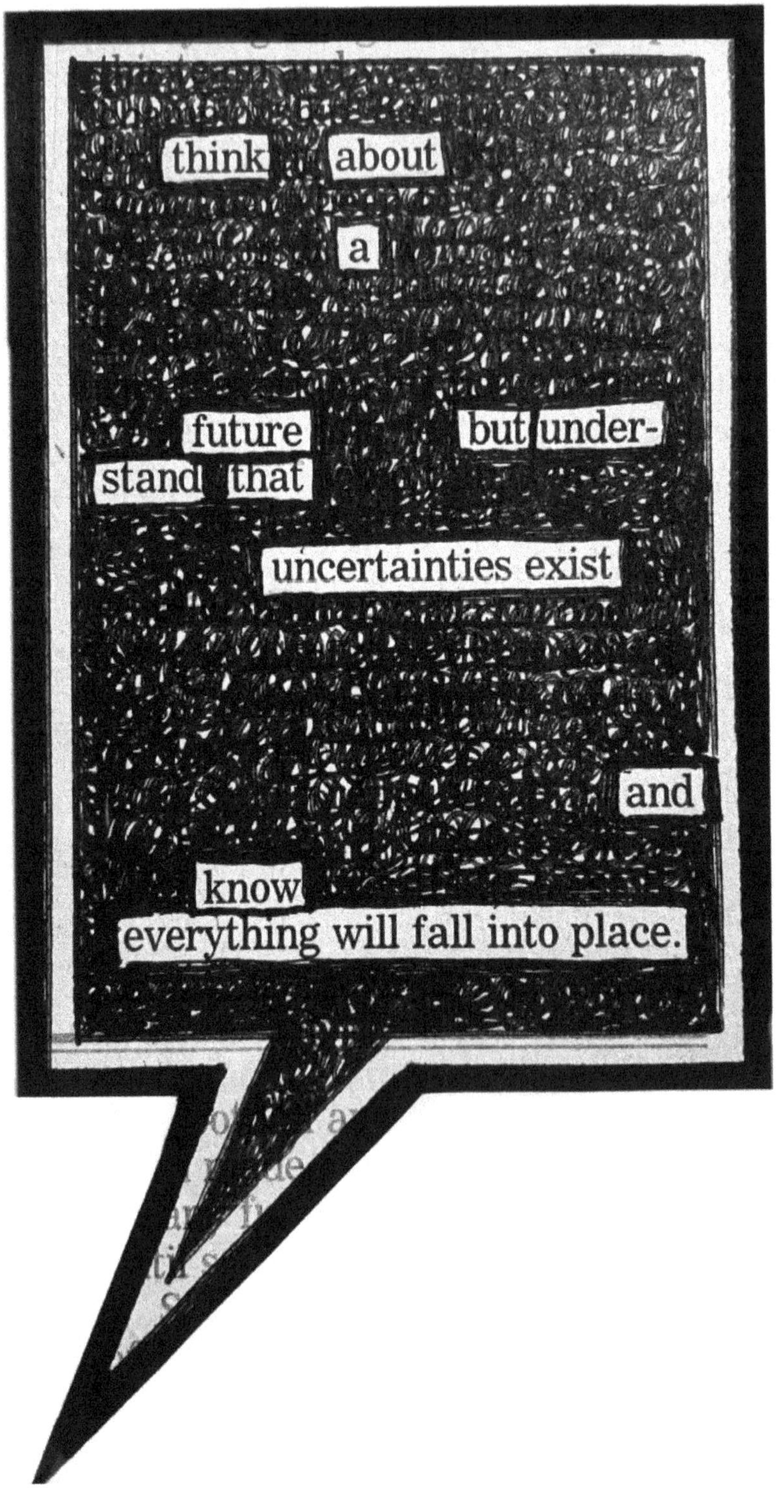
think about
a
future but under-
stand that
uncertainties exist
and
know
everything will fall into place.

Think about a future, but
understand that
uncertainties exist
and
know
everything
will fall into place.

Just downstream,
a good bridge,
welcoming.

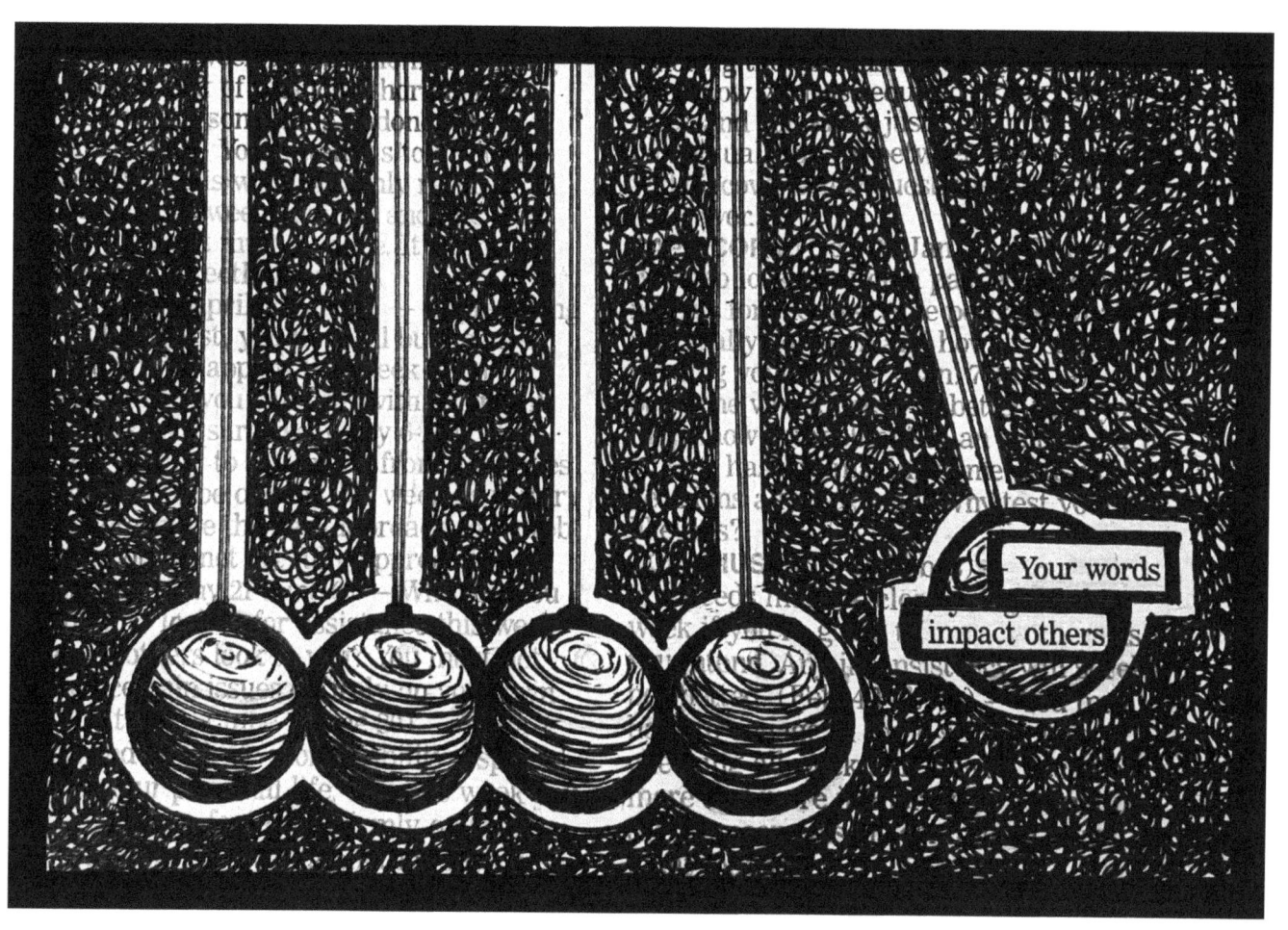

Your words
impact others.

his blue eyes

smiled.

there

on the road

gone to start a better life

gone to the ones who stayed

He claimed his ribbon of

tomorrow.

His blue eyes smiled
there on the road.

Gone to start a better life,
gone to the ones who stayed,

he claimed his ribbon of tomorrow.

A reason to celebrate—
to put it plainly:
morning will arrive.

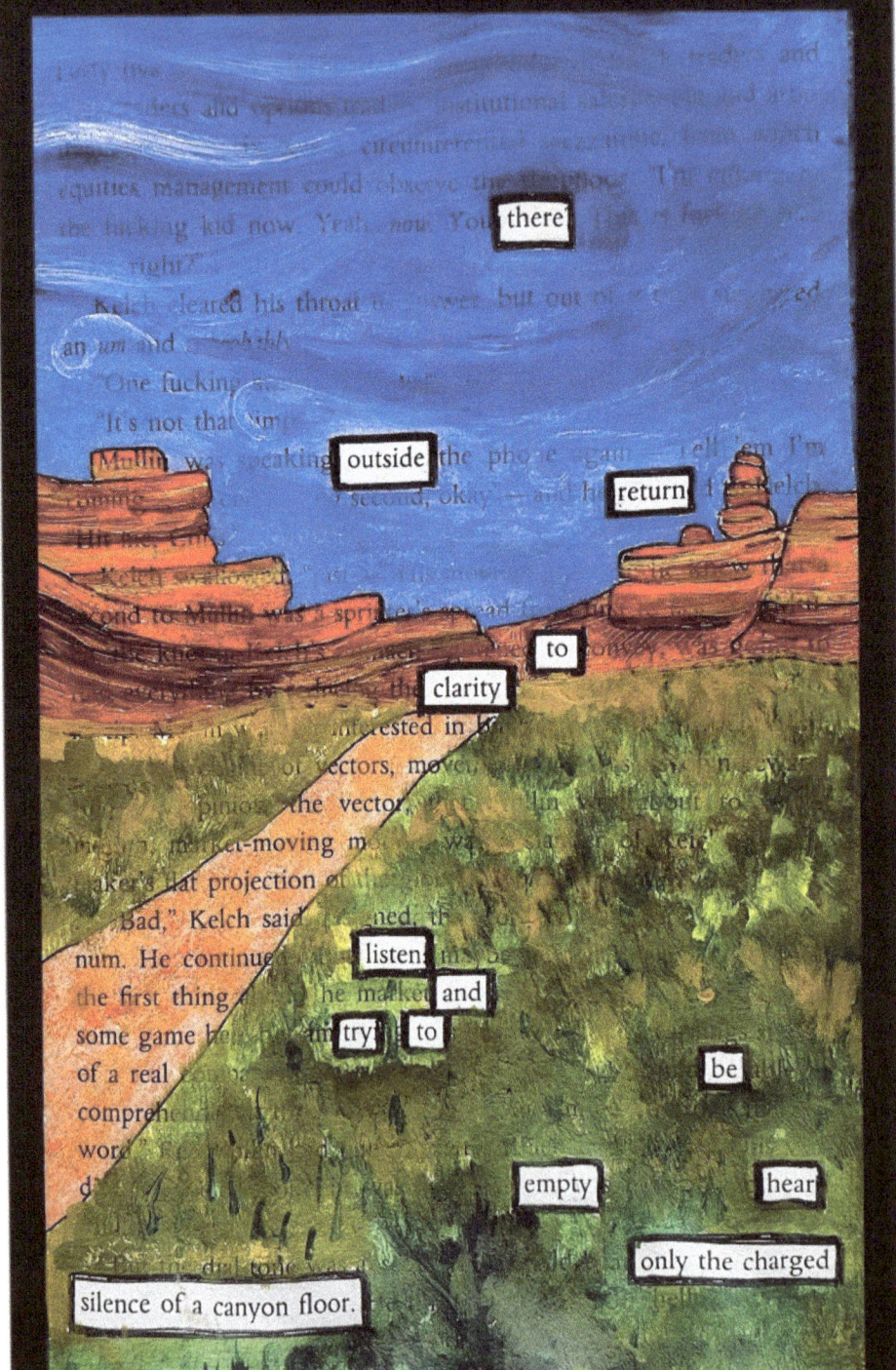

there

outside return

to

clarity

listen and
try to

be

empty hear

only the charged

silence of a canyon floor.

There, outside,
return to clarity.

Listen
and try to be empty.

Hear only
the charged silence
of a canyon floor.

smell like anything. Kelch scraped his fingertip across the beveled edge of the tabletop, leaving the *dotless* i's of a gravity. He picked up a napkin and wiped his mouth, apologetic in chair.

Nathanson rose with his now *wrapped* sandwich, "After that ..." He left, and Kim left, and Einstadt left, and Kelch figured that he would eat in his office after all.

2

Listen: two things are true, Kelch thought as he sat in his office, his palm mating with the mouse's plastic hump. Two things are true: A: nothing is happening, and B: it wasn't me, really me in the article. Because if something was happening, or if it was really him, Kelch would not have been able to breath clear-lunged now, to think ordered thoughts. A boa's vise of absurdity would have clamped him shut, and off. Nothing was happening, and he wouldn't allow it to happen—Kelch was an intimate of an unabsurd world—but as he reinforced the two truths, the inarguable deductive corollaries, the C and the D, did not come. Yes, Kelch thought, it largely follows that I have nothing to worry about or there will be no repercussions, or no one will find out, but those conclusions *largely* followed. They were fixed on the base truths with sloppy mortarwork; they were not Incan miracles stacked perfect without cement

For his *first* three years at Freshlit Feld, Kelch had worked for Veena Gupta. (He would have called her his mentor if she hadn't once said that only idiots needed mentors.) In the hiring interview, she had lectured that the key to security analysis, and by extension human thought, was a relentless pursuit of bits. "Do you *know* what bits are?" Um, yeah, sure, Kelch nodded, doglike. Veena continued, laying down four pillars of wisdom. One, the equity market is obviously not a binary system of yeses and nos. Two, nonetheless, all

In
the breath—
in
and
out—
lies
the key.

intuition

is

the

whispered suggestion

of

mind.

listen listen. listen

Intuition is
the whispered
suggestion
of mind.
Listen.
Listen.
Listen.

When I'm still,
I touch peace.

All the recipients of Kelch's voice mail message could translate every word with a trained, reflexive decoder. *I am not doing anything with my rating just yet.* Meaning: concentrate on "just yet" and don't be surprised if I lower my recommendation tomorrow or next week, take Tee-Fog off the Focus Buy list. *I am going to run the new numbers tonight through my model.* Meaning: I will put the new data in my model like every other analyst, but no alchemic insights will result. On the call—you heard—Mike Margion told everyone to lower their numbers by four cents per share for the year, and I will take my number down those commanded four fives if I am being conservative. Anyway, you and I know that for the next few weeks, maybe months, Tee-Fog will wriggle on the ground epileptically and any estimate of future earnings will be **ignore**d by the traders whipsaw-ing the stock on lot-sizes. For certainty, for salvation here might, certainty in the midst—lack salvation Margion Kelch had no idea whatnot do because he never even left his desk except the one of his emptiness, **the** the core of the **pounding fear of** his heart climbing up, above, up in his chest. The passion that fired it whispered its **doubt and dread** into the ear of every analyst of every investor. Kelch had for example loudly to buy Tee-Fog when it was six dollars, more, a share, **and** the stock was then more attractive now, at least on its current... he had... been wrong... six letter dollars wrong, that morning. So... should any... **believe** him now?

The... it... penny over and capital or trade... it was a field... for consuming portion... Kelch and looked, query and everyone... in... side... when sider sheets count in equity... the insomnia... and... Margion was upside down, just... or I die... the shareholder on... the edge. Who was to say that Tee-Fog couldn't still by some... edicts come from... Who was to say that their competitors... right... weren't slanting to slash prices by half. Who was to say that one's customers would not finally decide, this year, that they no longer needed a new candy bar, new car, another action movie. The next microchip... **in** **truth**... the knot of the paradox grew... gyrating... baby kicking, and

Ignore
the pounding fear
of doubt
and dread

and

believe
in
truth.

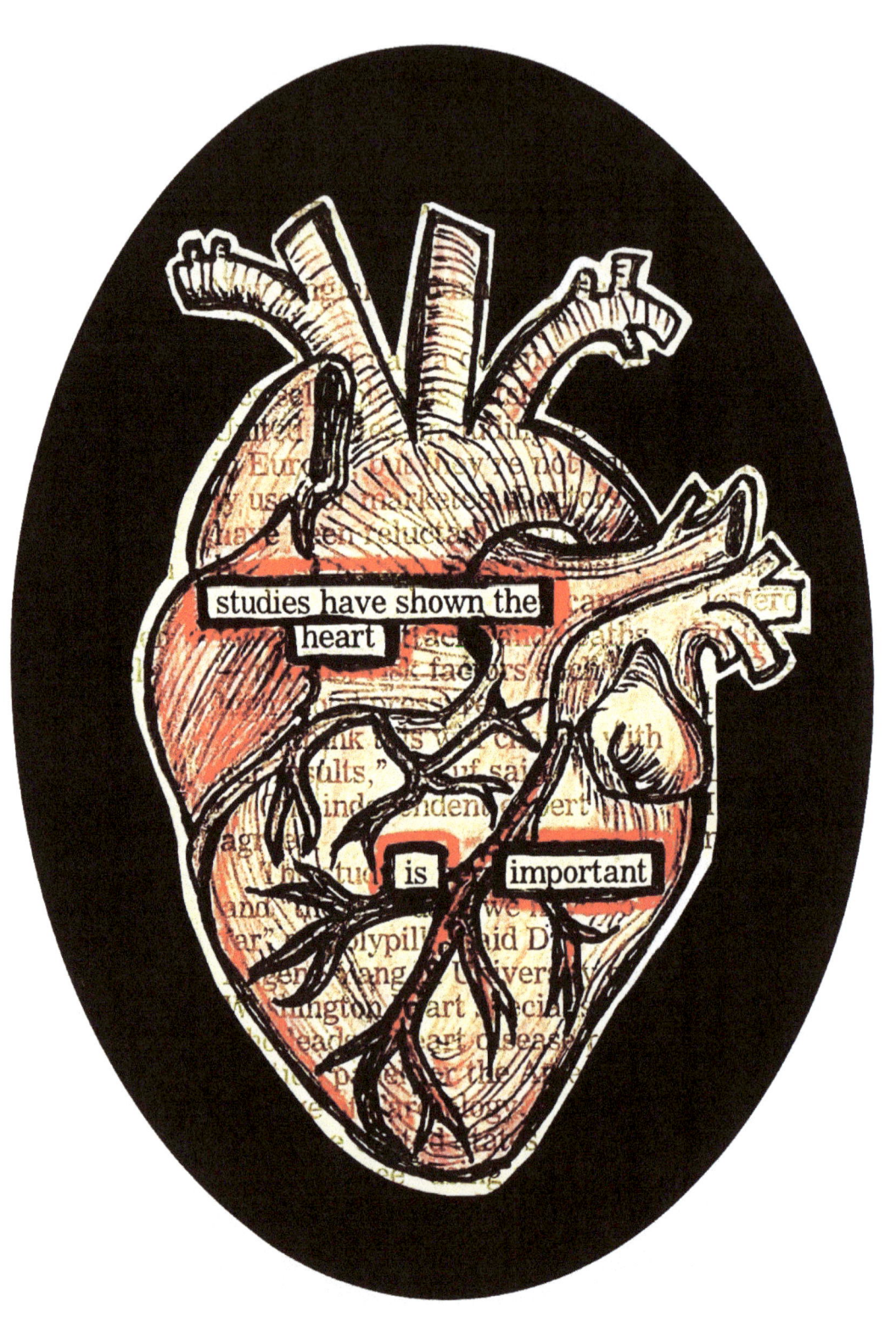

Studies have shown:
the heart
    is important.

...particles, which had already formed a constant coating on Kelch's sweaters, hair, youth, would deliver on their backs, up the warped stairs, the tuna smell to his room. Even a towel under the door wouldn't help. Kelch couldn't understand why he couldn't smell Kim's tuna now; the sanitation was only three feet away. And he couldn't understand why he couldn't smell his own grilled chicken or that aftershave crap that Nathanson wore. "That's tuna salad?" He then added, flatly, "Huh."

"Kimchi likes it," Nathanson winked at Emstadt, "because it remind him of Number Tree Sister." No one at the table...

laugh

laugh

laugh

| laugh |

...Nathanson... when, "You, by the way," he argued..., next slave on the sweet chain.

"She had," Kelch said, "until she found out that you had a little Jewish prick." Torvil and Nathanson could spend hours volleying racial cracks. Shot, it's tough being an oppressed minority in this firm. Return. I don't know how you got a job here at all, did you take a creative stab on your résumé? But Kim, still eager and oddly appreciative (after six years) to be a company victim would return. Only when Nathanson or Torvil laughed, and especially only... It didn't take much Jecum Lehr his eyes to narrow further, to buttonholes, and he would yell, with sluggish-tongue consonants, "Stop telling about my sisters or I'll kill you."

Everyone would [**then laugh even louder.**] At those times, Kelch suspected that he alone felt any sympathy for Kim, and he would feel relieved too, also curious and jealous. For no one seemed to remember, if anyone [**even**] knew, that he had a sister too, back in Rockford. They didn't know her name, they didn't joke about her, they didn't ask [**about**] her. The guy at Krechler probably had no players their colleagues either. Kelch thought, thirty, one, with three kids, [**troubles**], husband home by five-thirty every night.

After six years, Kelch had ceased the dead and repetition of back in Rockford, the contrasting, resolving *back in Rockford*. He had long...

Laugh!
Then laugh
    even louder—
        even
            about
                troubles.

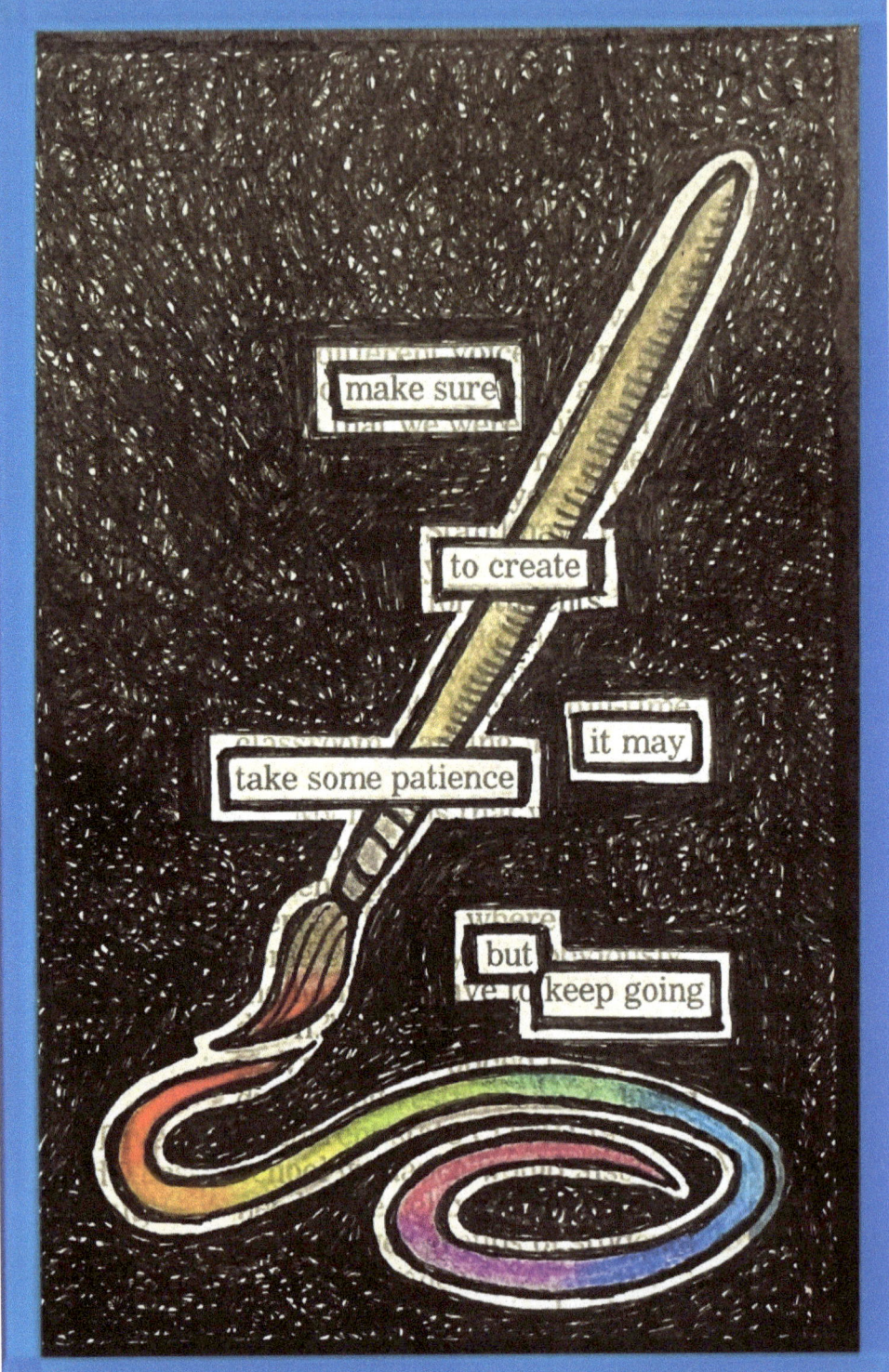

Make sure
to create.

It may take
some patience,
but
keep going.

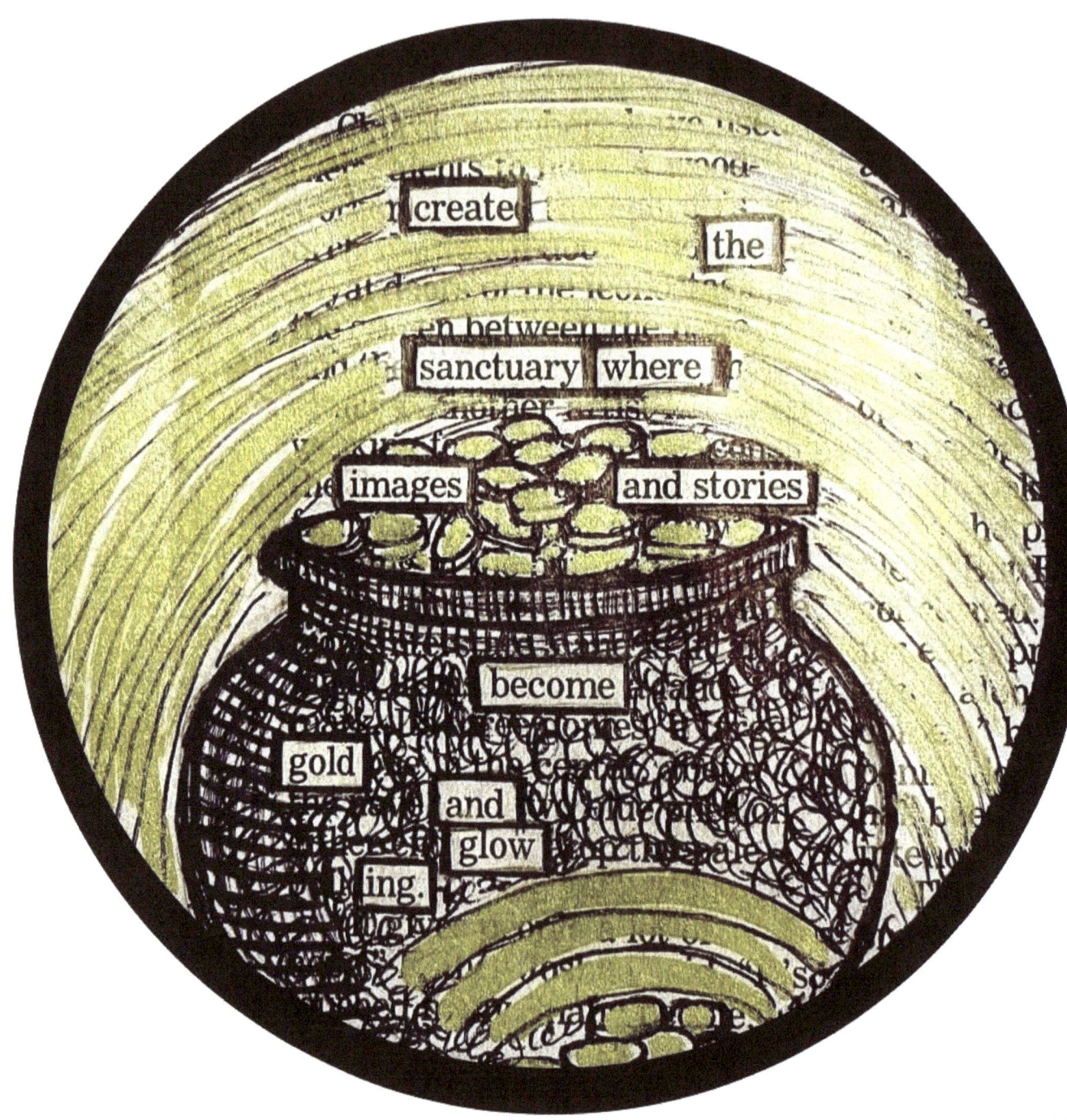

created the sanctuary where images and stories become gold and glowing.

Create the sanctuary
where images and stories
become
gold
and
glowing.

on the threshold of   some pleasant

afternoon

she lifts herself

to see whether she truly can use her wings   then

circles   in great joy

goes out into the wide world

excited and delighted with her achieve-

ment

and plays her part

courageous

as a

queen

at the height of her powers

On the threshold
of some pleasant afternoon
she lifts herself
to see
whether she
truly can use her wings, then
   circles in great joy,
    goes out into the wide world,
      excited and delighted
      with her achievement,
  and plays her part
        courageous as a queen
        at the height of her powers.

I have started flying again.

all over the place.

I have started
flying again,
all over the place.

Oft times in grass, on trees, in flight,
Sore accidents on you may light.
65 O to your safety have an eye,
So happy may you live and die:
Mean while my days in tunes I'll spend,
Till my weak lays with me shall end.
In shady woods I'll sit and sing,
70 And things that past, to mind I'll bring.
Once young and pleasant, as are you,
But former toys (no joys) adieu.
My age I will not once lament,
But sing my time so near is spent.
75 And from the top bough take my flight,
Into a country beyond sight,
Where old ones instantly grow young,
And there with seraphims[12] set song;
No seasons cold, nor storms they see,
80 But spring lasts to eternity.
When each of you shall in your nest
Among your young ones take your rest,
In chirping language oft them tell
You had a dam that lov'd you well,
85 That did what could be done for young,
And nurst you up till you were strong,
And 'fore she once would let you fly,
She show'd you joy and misery;
Taught what was good, and what was ill,
90 What would save life, and what would kill.
Thus gone, amongst you I still live,
And dead, yet speak, and counsel give:
Farewell, my birds, farewell adieu,
I happy am, if well with you.

1678

O so happy!

My days in tunes I'll spend:
I'll sing joy!

I will sing
    from the top bough
        and shall
            in chirping language
            tell you
                to fly!

Tell the story
you need to.

brighten

the worlds of the young and the old

one by one.

Sometimes all it takes to brighten someone's day is a
terrarium in a little jar, homemade and hand-delivered.
...
...together when seventh graders from...middle
school took a stroll to the Royale Gardens Health
& Rehabilitation Center, jar-sized terrariums in hand.
"...pretty honey," retired Albertsons checker
...McLean said to North student Dakata Johnson
when...she handed over the gift. "It's very pretty."
   Led by science teacher Le...Mon Iterson, the stu-
dents delivered the low-maintenance terrariums to will-
ing recipients, one by one.
   Assembling the terrariums served as an endcap to
the students' education on photosynthesis.

Brighten
the worlds
of the young
and the old
one
by
one.

Despite the difficulties,
believe in people.

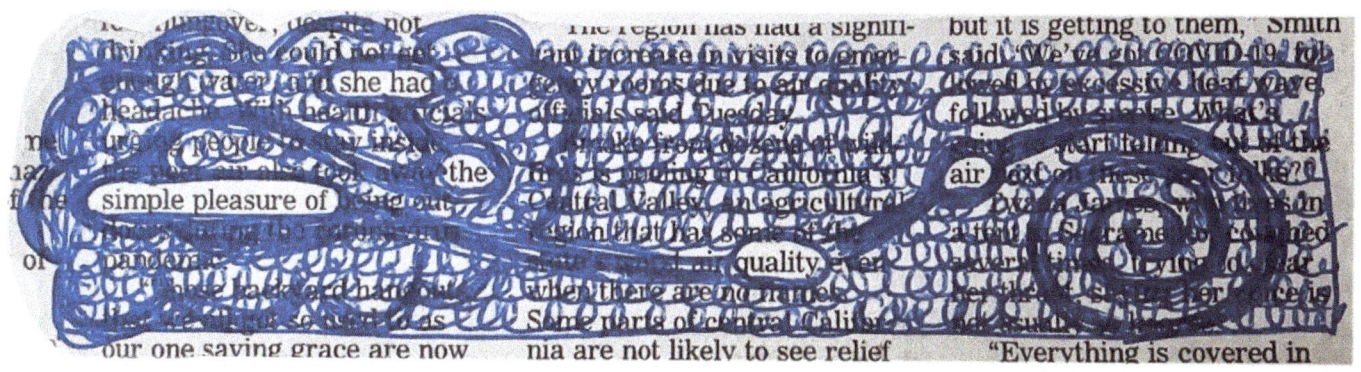

She had
the simple pleasure
of quality air.

gratitude

keeps us
connected

to
friends and strangers

which is the point

it

nourishes and helps us grow

Gratitude
keeps us connected
to friends and strangers,
which is the point:
It nourishes
and helps us grow.

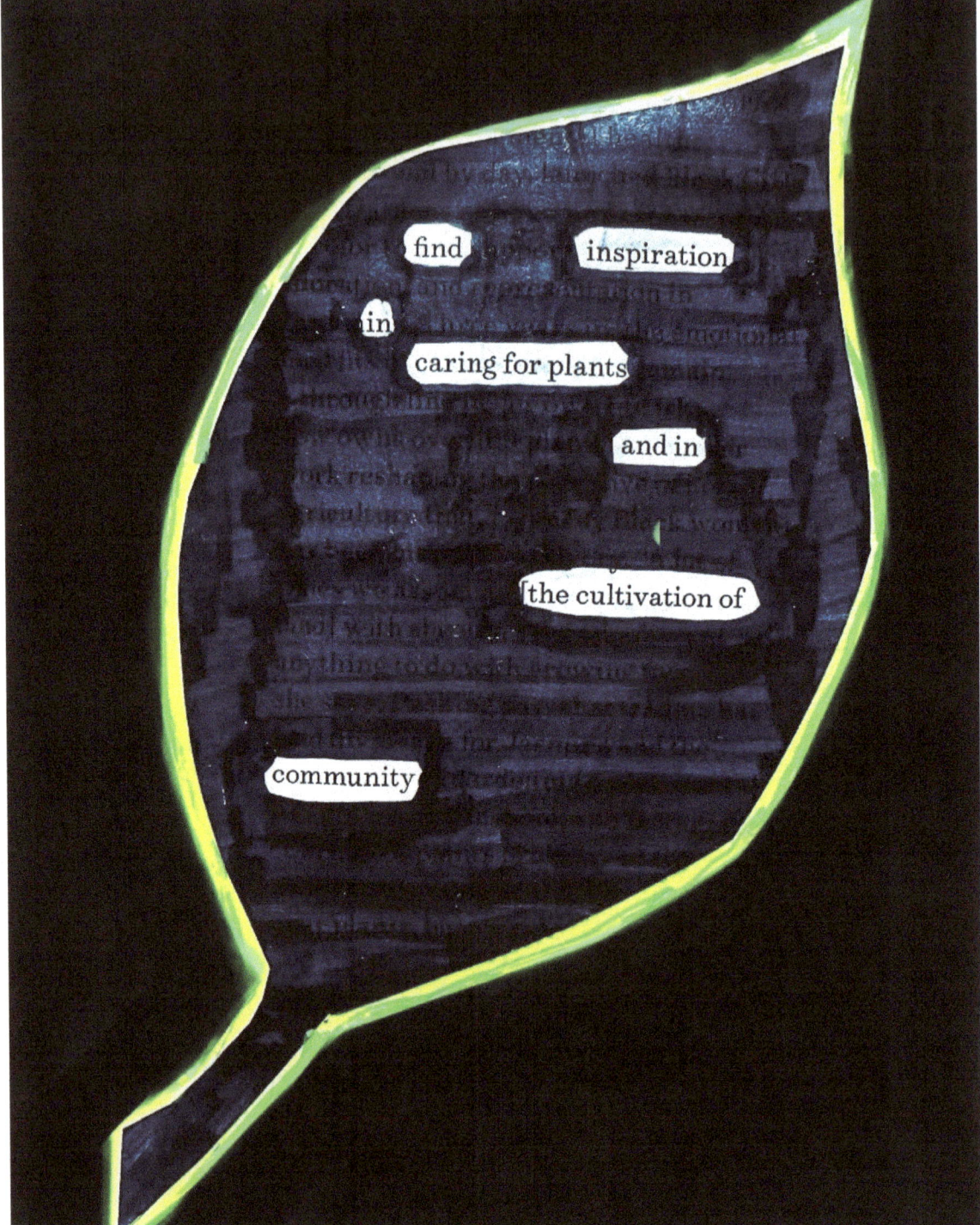

Find inspiration

in caring for plants

and

in the cultivation
of community.

In difficult times,
encouragement
and support
say *I know you.*

one
light begins

darkness

d
i
s
s
i
p
a
t
e
s

the world   mattered,

the

water

the air
all

of

it

The world mattered—
the water, the air—
all of it.

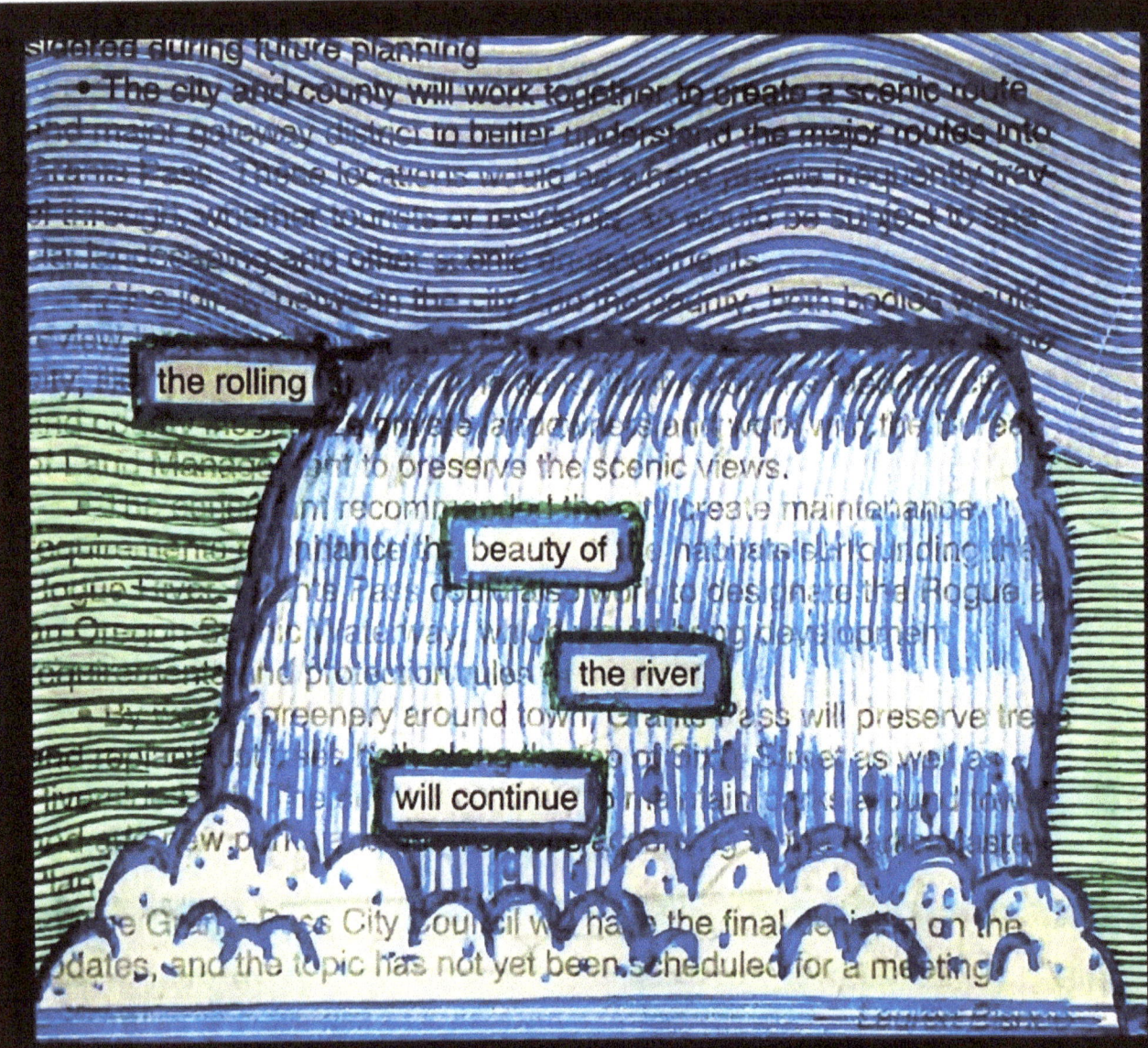

The rolling beauty
of the river
will continue.

Plant
trees
all over the world.

seeking shelter under a tree in the grass, surrounded by woods, She was home.

Seeking shelter
under a tree
in the grass
surrounded by woods,
she
    was

    home.

take time to relax.

autumn

is

in the wind.

today

all day

today

all day

Take time to relax.
Autumn is in the wind
today, all day
today, all day.

What's wrong
with rest?

the day

scattering

good
on the horizon

Retreat, s

West

The day,
scattering good
on the horizon,
retreats West.

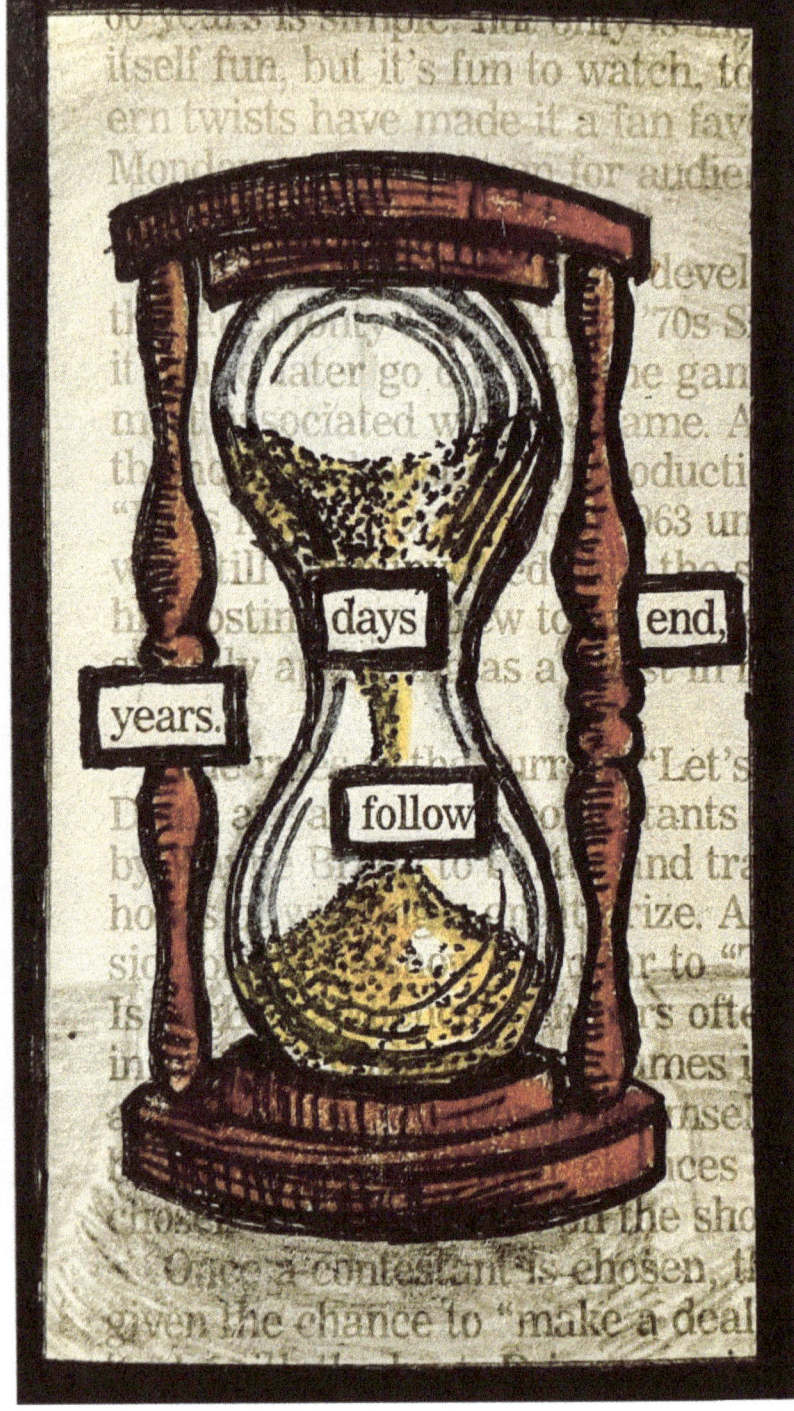

days   end,

years.

follow

Days end.
Years follow.

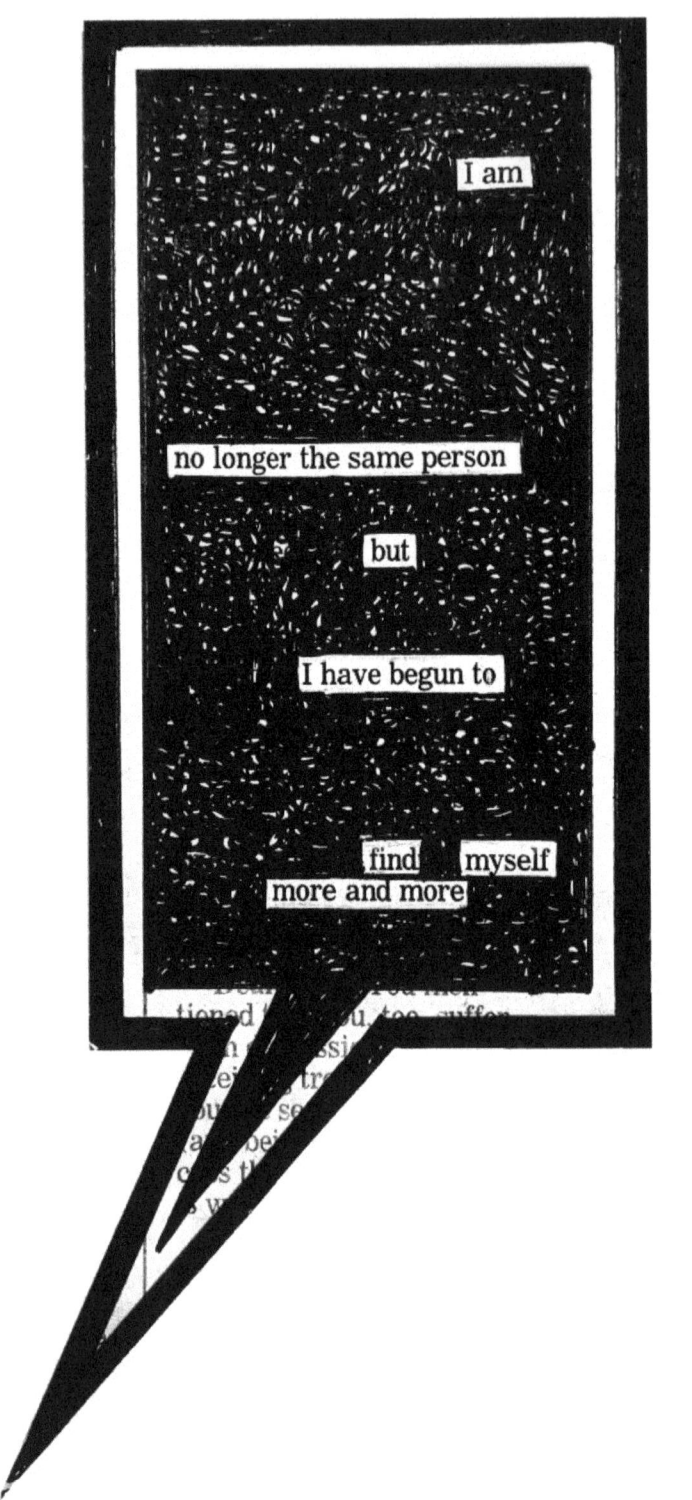

I am
no longer
the same person

but
I have begun
to find myself
more and more.

may you remain open, and fill your life with joy

May you
remain open
and
fill your life
with joy.

About the Poet and Artist

Jennifer Rood has been writing poems and stories since first grade, when her teacher would set aside time for her to read her work to the class. She has dozens of published poems in various journals and anthologies, including *Verseweavers*, *The Literary Hatchet*, *Slant*, *Snapdragon*, *GreenPrints*, *Frogpond*, and others. She is a past Board Member (2018 – 2021) and President (2020 – 2021) of the Oregon Poetry Association, and won first place for her prose poem "Breaking" in OPA's Fall 2022 Contest. In 2023, she released *What the Heart Says*, a hand-stitched chapbook of found poetry/art (available through

oregonbooks.com). After raising a family and working variously as a high school English, social studies, and art teacher for the past 30 years, she retired in the summer of 2023. In the fall of 2023, she served five weeks as the Artist in Residence at the Oregon Caves National Monument writing poetry inspired by the monument and its history. *Present and Speaking Everywhere* is her first full-length collection.

Printed in the USA
CPSIA information can be obtained
at www.ICGtesting.com
CBHW040202310124
3899CB00020B/204

9 781956 892420